C000110046

Cookies

Written by Malcolm Long

KUDOS

Published by Kudos, an imprint of Top That! Publishing plc.
Copyright © 2004 Top That! Publishing plc,
Tide Mill Way, Woodbridge, Suffolk, IPI2 IAP,
www.kudosbooks.com
Kudos is a Trademark of Top That! Publishing plc

Contents

Contents

Contents

There is something magical and evocative of childhood about making biscuits and cookies. However, very few commercially produced cookies, including even some of the very expensive varieties, can match baking your own.

Home-baked cookies are very simple to make and many have a lightness and crunch that is irresistible, with a flavour that is only possible from something lifted from your own oven. The smells of baking are hard to beat – who doesn't relish the delicious aromas of ginger, golden syrup, the zest of orange or lemons and the smell of almonds, as they pervade your home.

Wise estate agents suggest roasting coffee prior to showing prospective clients around houses that are for sale, but a baking batch of cookies will definitely clinch the deal. Most of us have made cookies at some time, whether it was at school or on a rainy Saturday afternoon helping mum. Eating your home-made treats may well play havoc with your waistline but baking them does wonders for stress and will make you very popular with friends and family.

This book includes a fantastic selection of traditional-style cookies but also contains great new ideas for sweet treats the whole family can enjoy: from bite-sized brownies to petit fours, meringues to sticky cereal delights and lots more that will really tantalise the taste buds.

Tips on Baking

As with most things, successful baking depends on many factors. It is certainly true that the very best results are always obtained from the finest and freshest ingredients and careful following of the recipes. It may well be possible to exchange some of the ingredients – for example cheaper varieties of margarine for butter – but unless you have a medical reason for doing this, the best ingredients tend to speak for themselves.

Great results will always be obtained from ingredients which are used at room temperature, unless the recipe tells you otherwise. Always store dry goods in clean, airtight containers which are labelled and dated, as many ingredients will deteriorate with age. Do not add fresh ingredients to old, always use up the older items first.

Try to stock a variety of ingredients: it is very frustrating to find that you cannot make something new and exciting because you are short of a few vital ingredients.

Oven temperatures

Gas Mark	Fahrenheit °F	Celsius °C
1/4	225	110
1/2	250	120
1	275	140
2	300	150
3	325	160
4	350	180
5	375	190
6	400	200
7	425	220
8	450	230
9	475	240

Weights and Measures

The following chart provides approximate conversions of weight which have been rounded up or down for practical use. When following a recipe use one set of measurements – ounces or grams – throughout to maintain the correct ratios.

Ounces	Grams
1	30
2	60
3	90
4	120
5	150
6	180
7	210
8	240
9	270
10	300
11	330
12	360
13	390
14	420
15	450
16 (1 lb)	480

Equipment

Baking cookies doesn't require an armada of tools and equipment, but you will need the essentials such as reliable kitchen scales, mixing bowls and a rolling pin. The following should also be noted to ensure your efforts run smoothly and achieve the best results:

Try to have several different sieves. Whenever possible, sieve flours and fine sugars, or anything which may develop lumps, prior to use.

Many of us won't have the luxury of a large kitchen, but aim to work tidily and give yourself the maximum space you can afford. Clear up as you go along. This will allow you to enjoy the fruits of your labour without being confronted with a sink full of washing-up.

Remember the basic rules of hygiene: wash your hands before starting and between handling different ingredients and stages. Many tasks are much better performed manually but hands are just like any other kitchen tool and must be kept clean.

Try to keep some good sharp knives to work with. Blunt knives are dangerous as you have to apply too much pressure to cut with them, and slips are more likely to cause damage to misplaced fingers.

Always use a clean chopping board for cutting. Cutting directly onto Formica work surfaces will scratch them and blunt your knives.

Choose large mixing bowls which may appear larger than necessary, but will allow you to beat or whisk without the ingredients being splashed around the kitchen. If you have the kitchen space, there are various kitchen gadgets you might find useful: including food processors, mixing machines, liquidisers or hand-held electric whisks – all of which can save you time and a lot of arm ache.

Cooking Tips

Ovens

If you are going to do a lot of baking then a large oven, preferably forced air or fan assisted is best, since these will allow food to brown evenly in all parts of the oven.

With a conventional non-assisted oven, it is safer to use only the top two shelves and to keep baking trays at least 2–3 cm apart to allow heat to circulate. You will need to swap the trays around to ensure even cooking and browning. Try also to keep them away from the walls or door of the oven to avoid the food burning.

Baking sheets and trays

It is a good idea to buy the best baking sheets and trays you can afford. There are many varieties of non-stick trays to choose from and these are very useful and effective. However, heat-proof rubber matting and moulds are now widely available in many shapes and sizes; they are extremely easy to use and give great results. Although expensive, they are very effective when used in or out of the oven. A cheaper alternative is silicone paper which is reusable if not burnt and can be cut to any size quite easily.

Whichever baking trays you choose, they should be flat with very low sides to allow the heat to travel evenly across the food being cooked.

Cooking Tips

 ## Temperatures

The temperatures given in this book are approximate since no two ovens are ever the same. It is also true that however strictly you follow the recipe, the mixtures will always vary slightly.

 ## Cooking times

To test whether cookies are done, first check the colour. Most biscuits are cooked when they have reached a pale, golden colour. The colour test won't be applicable to all recipes, so instead try to slide the cookies on the tray: if they slide they are normally ready.

Biscuits that are still warm are normally still flexible and should be allowed to cool on wire racks to crisp before being stored. Biscuits which are to be rolled or shaped need to be formed before they cool; if they harden, a few seconds in a warm oven will soften them and allow for reshaping.

 ## Storage

If biscuits are to be kept for any length of time they are better stored uncooked. This is done by shaping them in the usual way on a baking sheet but placing them in the freezer instead of in the oven. When the biscuits are set, remove from the baking sheets and store between layers of cling film in a plastic box in the freezer. Cooked biscuits should always be kept in an airtight container.

The Stock Ingredients used in Baking

Flour

Self-raising flour – usually medium strength flour, which is combined with baking powder (use 10 g baking powder to 450 g flour). May be used in biscuit recipes but more frequently used in cake making.

Wholemeal flour – uses the whole of the wheat and contains the embryo germ (bran is the endosperm).

Cornflour – this is ground or milled from maize and is mostly starch. Used as a thickening agent for jellies and custards, it is included in some cake and biscuit recipes.

Arrowroot – virtually pure starch and used for glazes as it is very clear when cooked.

Rice flour – finely ground rice used in shortbreads and macaroons, either to save on almonds, or to add texture to the mixture.

Sugar

Sugar has various uses, the most obvious is as a sweetener. However in cakes, combined with fat and eggs, it helps hold air. In rubbed-in mixtures and pastries it makes the mixture lighter in texture. Sugar also makes a wonderful preservative because moulds and bacteria will not thrive in concentrated sugar solutions.

You will find a wide range of sugars in the supermarkets. The following list summarises their uses in baking and cooking generally.

Granulated sugar – refined white sugar with large or coarse granules. A multi-purpose sugar used for sweetening; the most economical sugar.

The Stock Ingredients used in Baking

Castor sugar – finer than granulated, and used mostly in cakes, pastries, puddings and cookies.

Icing sugar – white sugar ground to a fine powder that is used for icing, cake decorating and for dusting before and after cooking.

Demerara sugar – honey coloured sugar with large crystals, which has a sandy texture; ideal for cooking.

Barbados or dark, moist sugar – often used where a dark colour is needed and its characteristic toffee flavour is used to mask the bitter flavour of bicarbonate of soda.

Sand sugar – rather like demerara but pale brown and very soft. Can be used in place of demerara.

Eggs

The eggs used in the following recipes, unless stated otherwise, are medium and refer to chicken's eggs weighing approximately 60 g. Many of the recipes call for separated eggs: this can be achieved with a small piece of equipment designed specifically for the purpose. It is rather like small, round bowl, usually metallic, with a small slot cut in one wall fairly low down. When an egg is broken into the bowl the white of the egg will escape through the slot in the side leaving the yolk behind. This can also be achieved manually by tipping a shelled egg into the hand and allowing the white to escape through the fingers, leaving the yolk cupped in the hand.

Testing the freshness of an egg is an easy task: a fresh egg, when placed in cold water, will sink to the bottom of the container. If the egg is slightly less fresh it will start to rise towards the surface with the round side uppermost. The higher the egg floats the older it is, if the egg floats clear it is most likely to be rotten and should be discarded.

Butter versus margarine

Butter is the preferred choice in most of the recipes in this book, but it is possible to substitute it with margarine. Soft margarines are very easy to use, especially for creaming (for the same results when using block butter or margarine it is necessary to allow them to reach room temperature before use), and margarines are arguably healthier than butter. It is also true to say that margarines which are prepared for baking will usually give a better result in all aspects except flavour – the best of which is always achieved when using butter.

Almond Maraschino Biscuits

ingredients

30 g (1 oz) nibbed almonds
120 g (4 oz) plain flour
30 g (1 oz) ground almonds
60 g (2 oz) caster sugar
60 g (2 oz) butter
1 egg yolk
2 tsps maraschino liqueur

maraschino icing

90 g (3 oz) icing sugar
1 tbsp maraschino liqueur
2 tbsp hot water

makes

Approximately 25 biscuits

Preheat the oven to 180°C. Toast the nibbed almonds until golden brown. Mix the sieved flour, ground almonds and sugar in a large bowl and rub in the butter until the mixture resembles fine breadcrumbs. Add the egg yolk and maraschino liqueur and mix together to form a dough.

Allow to rest for 10 minutes then roll out on a lightly floured surface until approximately 4 mm thick. Cut into rounds using a 6 cm (2 1/2 inch) fluted cutter and place on baking sheets lined with silicone paper. Bake for 10–12 minutes or until pale, golden brown. Allow to cool on wire racks.

To make the maraschino icing: sift the icing sugar into a clean bowl, add the maraschino liqueur and hot water, and stir until smooth, adding more water if required. Spoon a little icing into the centre of each biscuit and smooth out to the edges. Sprinkle the toasted almonds on top.

Almond Chocolate Fingers

Preheat the oven to 180°C. In a large bowl, soften the butter and beat in the ground almonds and sugar. Using an electric hand blender, beat in the eggs and stir in the sieved flour.

Line a baking tray (approximately 30 cm/12 inches square) with silicone paper. Spread the mixture evenly over the tray and bake for 8–10 minutes until golden brown. While still warm, use a sharp knife to cut into three 10 cm (4 inch) strips.

To make the topping: melt the butter, sugar and glucose in a pan over a medium heat. Add the water and flaked almonds and stir until the sugar has dissolved. Bring to the boil and simmer for 4–5 minutes.

Spread the topping over the warm biscuit base, and bake in the oven for a further 5–6 minutes, or until the topping is golden brown. When cool enough to handle, cut into fingers and leave to cool further on a wire rack.

Melt the chocolate in a clean bowl over a pan of boiling water. Carefully dip the biscuits diagonally in the melted chocolate and place on silicone paper until set. Store in an airtight container.

ingredients

60 g (2 oz) butter
120 g (4 oz) ground almonds
120 g (4 oz) caster sugar
2 eggs
2 tbsp plain flour

topping

60 g (2 oz) butter
75 g (2 1/2 oz) sugar
75 g (2 1/2 oz) liquid glucose
2 tbsp water
120 g (4 oz) flaked almonds
120 g (4 oz) dark chocolate

serves

Approximately 30 biscuits

Crunchy Apricot Sticks

ingredients

120 g (4 oz) butter
120 g (4 oz) brown sugar
$1/2$ tbsp vanilla essence
1 egg
75 g (2 $1/2$ oz) self-raising flour
$1/2$ tsp salt
90 g (3 oz) wheatgerm
60 g (2 oz) desiccated coconut
60 g (2 oz) rolled oats
120 g (4 oz) dried apricots, chopped
60 g (2 oz) cornflakes
120 g (4 oz) dark chocolate

makes

Approximately 25 biscuits

Preheat the oven to 180°C. Cream the butter, brown sugar, vanilla essence and egg together in a bowl. Stir in the sieved flour, salt, wheatgerm, coconut, rolled oats, chopped apricots and cornflakes and mix well. Take one tablespoon of mixture, roll it gently in your hands to form a finger and place on a baking sheet lined with silicone paper. Flatten slightly to firm. Repeat with rest of the mixture and bake for 10–12 minutes. Leave to cool on wire racks.

Meanwhile, melt the chocolate in a bowl over a pan of boiling water. Dip the bases into the melted chocolate and drizzle some chocolate over the biscuits.

Apricot and Pistachio Biscuits

ingredients

60 g (2 oz) almond marzipan
90 g (3 oz) butter
2 tsp grated lime zest
1 tbsp lime juice
60 g (2 oz) caster sugar
1 egg, separated
150 g (5 oz) plain flour
1 tsp water
60 g (2 oz) flaked almonds
30 g (1 oz) chopped pistachio nuts
60 g (2 oz) apricot jam

makes

Approximately 25 biscuits

Preheat the oven to 180°C. Combine the marzipan, butter, lime zest and juice, sugar and egg yolk in a large bowl. Sift the flour into the mixture and knead gently until firm. Refrigerate for 20–30 minutes.

Roll out on a floured surface until 1 cm (1/2 inch) thick and cut into rounds with a 5 cm (2 inch) fluted cutter. Place on a baking sheet lined with silicone paper. Mix the egg white and water together and brush over the top of the biscuits before sprinkling with flaked almonds and chopped pistachios. Bake for 10–15 minutes until pale golden brown. Leave to cool, then brush with sieved apricot jam and return to the oven to glaze for 2–3 minutes. When cold, store in an airtight container.

Coffee and Hazelnut Biscotti

ingredients

120 g (4 oz) caster sugar
1 beaten egg
100 g (3 1/2 oz) plain flour
1 tbsp instant coffee
1/2 tsp vanilla essence
1/2 tbsp baking powder
120 g (4 oz) hazelnuts, toasted
   and chopped roughly
120 g (4 oz) white chocolate

makes

Approximately 20 biscuits

Reduce the oven temperature to 160°C and use a very sharp, serrated knife to cut thin slices diagonally. Place on baking sheets lined with silicone paper. Bake for a further 10–15 minutes until crisp, turning half way. Cool on wire racks. Meanwhile, melt the white chocolate in a bowl over a pan of hot water. When the biscotti have cooled, carefully cover one side of each cookie with chocolate and leave to set.

Preheat the oven to 180°C. Beat the sugar and egg together in a bowl and stir in the sieved flour, coffee, vanilla essence, baking powder and nuts to form a dough. Roll into a small, slightly flattened, loaf shape and bake for approximately 25 minutes covered with foil. Remove the foil and allow to stand until cool.

Soy and Cheese Savouries with Coconut and Chillies

ingredients
120 g (4 oz) Cheddar cheese
120 g (4 oz) butter
150 g (5 oz) plain flour
1 tbsp light soy sauce
1 tsp red chillies, finely chopped
60 g (2 oz) desiccated coconut

makes
Approximately 25 biscuits

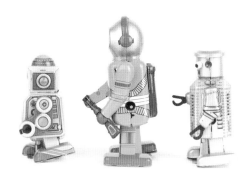

Preheat the oven to 180°C. Grate the cheese and combine with the butter, sieved flour and soy sauce in a bowl. Mix the chillies and the coconut together in a separate bowl. Roll tablespoons of the cheese mixture into balls and then roll in the coconut chilli mix. Place on a baking tray and press gently to flatten into rounds, then cook until crisp and golden. When cold, store in an airtight tin.

Sun-dried Tomato, Bacon and Black Olive Cookies

Preheat the oven to 190°C. Roast the bacon on a baking sheet until crisp, then finely chop and put to one side. Beat the butter in a bowl until soft before adding the egg yolk and cheese, and mix well. Stir in the sun-dried tomatoes and olives then mix in the flour, salt and cayenne to form into a firm dough. Wrap in cling film, and chill in the refrigerator until firm.

Roll out on a floured surface to approximately 5 mm thick, and cut with a 5 cm (2 inch) fluted cutter. Place the rounds on silicone paper, brush with water and scatter with the Parmesan cheese and chopped bacon.

Bake for 10–12 minutes, or until golden brown. Cool on a wire rack and then store in an airtight container.

Curry, Lime and Chilli Twists

ingredients

450 g (15 oz) pre-rolled puff pastry
120 g (4 oz) butter, melted
Zest of 1 lime, finely grated
1 tsp red chillies, finely chopped
30 g (1 oz) salted peanuts,
  finely crushed
2 tsp medium madras curry powder

makes

25–30 biscuits

Preheat the oven to 190°C. Lay out the sheets of pre-rolled puff pastry and cut into 1 cm (1/2 inch) strips. Brush with melted butter and sprinkle with the grated lime zest, chopped chillies, crushed peanuts and curry powder. Gently press the mixture into the pastry and twist the strips into a curl and place on baking sheets lined with silicone paper. Leave to rest for 20 minutes in the refrigerator before baking for 10–12 minutes, or until golden and crisp. Store in an airtight container.

Funny Face Biscuits

ingredients

120 g (4 oz) butter
120 g (4 oz) caster sugar
1 tsp vanilla essence
1 egg, lightly beaten
240 g (8 oz) plain flour
Egg white
Assorted sweets

makes

25–30 biscuits

Preheat the oven to 200°C. Cream the butter and sugar until light and fluffy. Gradually beat in the vanilla essence and egg, then gently fold in the flour and mix to a smooth dough. Cover with cling film and chill until firm (about 1 hour).

Roll out the dough until it is about 5 mm thick then, using a fluted, round cutter 6 cm (2¹/₂ inches) in diameter, cut out the biscuits and arrange on silicone paper. Bake in the oven for 6–10 minutes. Cool for 5 minutes by placing on a wire rack.

To make the funny faces you will need an unbeaten egg white, a selection of children's sweets such as coloured liquorice bootlaces, glacé cherries, angelica and food colours. Use scraps of dough to make hair, moustaches and beards. Sweets can be used to make eyes, cheeks, lips and noses – all of which can be fixed in place using a little egg white brushed onto the biscuits before they are cooked. Alternatively, decorate after baking and secure the features in place using a paste of icing sugar and water.

Butter-iced Fancies

ingredients

120 g (4 oz) butter
120 g (4 oz) caster sugar
1 tsp vanilla essence
1 egg lightly beaten
120 g (4 oz) plain flour

butter icing

120 g (4 oz) butter
1 tsp vanilla essence
240 g (8 oz) icing sugar
1 tbsp milk
Various food colourings
Various sweets, chocolate,
  glacé fruits and nuts

makes

25–30 biscuits

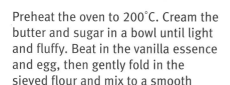

Preheat the oven to 200°C. Cream the butter and sugar in a bowl until light and fluffy. Beat in the vanilla essence and egg, then gently fold in the sieved flour and mix to a smooth dough. Cover with cling film and chill until firm (about 1 hour). Roll out the dough on a floured surface to approximately 5 mm thick. Using a round, fluted cutter, 6 cm (2$1/2$ inches) in diameter, cut cookie rounds and arrange on silicone paper, and bake for 6–10 minutes. Cool for 5 minutes by placing on a wire rack.

Beat the butter until soft, beat in the vanilla essence, milk and icing sugar until stiff and at piping consistency. Add a food colouring of your choice. Use a piping tool or bag to produce shapes and patterns with butter icing, then decorate with the various sweets, chocolates, fruits or nuts. The fun part for children is to use a range of exciting and different toppings to decorate the butter icing. Vary the biscuits by using differently shaped cutters or by adding flavourings to the butter icing.

ingredients

120 g (4 oz) butter
90 g (3 oz) brown sugar
1 egg yolk
1 tsp bicarbonate of soda
4 tsp ground ginger
360 g (12 oz) flour
2 tbsp golden syrup
120g (4 oz) dark chocolate

makes

Makes about 10–15

Preheat the oven to 180°C. Cream the butter and sugar together in a bowl until light and fluffy. Carefully work in the egg yolk, then add the sieved bicarbonate of soda, ginger and flour, and mix well. Add the syrup to form a dough; knead until smooth, then divide into five or six pieces.

Roll each piece into a ball and sandwich between two sheets of silicone paper. Using a rolling pin, roll over the top of the sheets to form an even layer approximately 1 cm ($1/2$ inch) thick.

Carefully remove the top sheet of paper and place the bottom sheet on a baking tray. Use a gingerbread person cutter to cut out the biscuit, then carefully peel away the waste from the dough leaving the people shapes on the paper. Bake for 10–12 minutes then slide on to a wire rack to cool.

Meanwhile, melt the chocolate over a pan of hot water. Dip the legs and heads into the chocolate, for shoes and hair, leave on silicone paper to set. Use the remaining chocolate in a piping bag to add the smaller features such as eyes, buttons and belts, leave to set completely.

ingredients

120 g (4 oz) butter
120 g (4 oz) caster sugar
1 egg
240 g (8 oz) plain flour
Assorted sweets

royal icing

1 egg white
120 g (4 oz) icing sugar
Various food colourings

water icing

100 g (4 oz) icing sugar
1–2 tbsp water
Various food colourings

makes

Makes 20–30 cookies

Preheat the oven to 180°C. Cream the butter and sugar together in a bowl, until light and fluffy. Add the egg and mix well. Sift the flour into the creamed mixture and, using your hands, create a smooth, firm dough. Refrigerate the mixture for 15 minutes.

Roll the dough out on a floured surface until 5 mm thick. Using either a sharp knife or cutters, cut out various shapes and transfer to a greased baking tray. Bake in the oven for 10 minutes or until golden brown. Cool the cookies on wire racks.

Meanwhile, prepare the icings. Make the royal icing by lightly beating the egg white. Add the sieved icing sugar and beat until the mixture thickens. Separate into different bowls and add various food colourings as desired. Transfer to a piping tool or bag ready to decorate the biscuits. To make the water icing simply add enough water to make a thick, smooth paste. Spread the water icing over the cookies with a palette knife or spoon, then pipe the royal icing on for finer details. Decorate with additional sweets if desired.

Chocolate and Coconut Wheatie Crunch

ingredients

120 g (4 oz) butter
120 g (4 oz) brown sugar
1 egg
30 g (1 oz) wheatgerm
60 g (2 oz) desiccated coconut
120 g (4 oz) plain flour
60 g (2 oz) self-raising flour
120 g (4 oz) plain chocolate

makes

25–30 biscuits

Preheat the oven to 180°C. Cream the butter and sugar together in a bowl. Beat in the egg then gently fold in the wheatgerm, coconut and sieved flours. Mix well and form balls using heaped teaspoons of mixture rolled between your palms, then place on silicone paper.

Use the back of a knife blade to slightly flatten the balls, then bake for 10 minutes or until golden and crisp. Transfer to wire racks to cool.

Meanwhile, melt the chocolate over a pan of simmering water, and dip the cooled biscuits halfway into the chocolate. Allow to set on a cooling rack. Store in an airtight container when the chocolate has completely set.

Chocolate Chip Cookies

ingredients

90 g (3 oz) butter
90 g (3 oz) caster sugar
120 g (4 oz) self-raising flour
2 tsp cocoa powder
90 g (3 oz) chocolate chips
120 ml (4 fl oz) milk

makes

20 cookies

Preheat the oven to 180°C. Cream the butter and sugar together in a bowl, until light and fluffy. Sift the flour and cocoa powder into the creamed mixture and stir well. Add two-thirds of the chocolate chips and the milk, mixing in small quantities at a time.

Place teaspoons of the cookie dough on a greased baking tray. Sprinkle the remaining chocolate chips on top, and bake in the oven for 15–20 minutes or until golden. Leave to cool for 2 minutes on the tray before lifting onto a wire rack to cool completely.

Chocolate and Ginger Squares

ingredients

60 g (2 oz) butter
1 tbsp sugar
1 tsp vanilla essence
2 tbsp hazelnuts, chopped
1 tsp ground ginger
2 egg yolks
120 g (4 oz) plain flour
1 tbsp cocoa

topping

2 eggs
180 g (6 oz) brown sugar
30 g (1 oz) self-raising flour
1 tsp vanilla essence
90 g (3 oz) desiccated coconut
60 g (2 oz) chopped hazelnuts
30 g (1 oz) stem ginger,
  finely chopped
90 g (3 oz) dark chocolate

makes

18 biscuits

Preheat the oven to 180°C. Cream the butter and sugar together in a bowl until light and fluffy. Add the vanilla essence, hazelnuts, ginger and egg yolks, and mix well. Sift the plain flour and cocoa into the mixture and fold in until well blended. Line a 30 x 15 cm (12 x 6 inch) baking tin with 3 cm (1 1/4 inch) sides with silicone paper and roll the paste into the tin, press to fit.

To make the topping: beat the eggs and sugar together in a bowl until fluffy. Fold in the sieved self-raising flour and add the vanilla essence and coconut. Spread the topping over the biscuit base and scatter with chopped hazelnuts and stem ginger. Bake for 20–25 minutes or until cooked. Cool thoroughly before cutting into 5 cm (2 inch) squares. Melt the chocolate over a pan of simmering water, and decorate the top of the biscuits.

Chocolate and Coconut Rum Bars

ingredients

300 g (10 oz) dark chocolate
180 g (6 oz) butter, melted
4 tbsp golden syrup
3 tbsp coconut flavoured rum
180 g (6 oz) digestive biscuits
30 g (1oz) desiccated coconut
45 g (1 1/2 oz) chopped pecans
30 g (1 oz) chopped pistachios
60 g (2 oz) chopped glacé cherries
30 g (1 oz) white chocolate

makes

24 biscuits

Melt the dark chocolate over a pan of hot water, then add the melted butter, golden syrup, and coconut flavoured rum and stir until blended. Crush the digestive biscuits and add, along with the desiccated coconut, chopped nuts and the glacé cherries, to the chocolate mix, and stir vigorously.

Spoon the mixture into a square 20 cm (8 inch) cake tin lined with silicone paper and press lightly with a palette knife to smooth. Allow it to set for 2–3 hours then cut into rectangles. Melt the white chocolate in a bowl over a pan of simmering water, and drizzle over the biscuits to decorate.

Double Chocolate Orange Cookies

ingredients

150 g (5 oz) unsalted butter, softened
60 g (2 oz) light brown sugar
240 g (8 oz) plain flour
50 g (2 oz) unsweetened cocoa powder
2 tsp baking powder
75 g (2 1/2 oz) dark chocolate, chopped
Grated zest of 2 oranges
2 tbsp orange juice

makes

30 cookies

Preheat the oven to 180°C. Line two baking trays with baking parchment. Beat the butter and sugar together in a bowl, until pale and fluffy. Sift the flour, cocoa and baking powder together twice and then carefully fold into the butter and sugar mixture. Add the chopped chocolate, orange zest and orange juice and gently mix together to form a smooth dough.

On a lightly-floured surface, roll out the dough to a thickness of 1/2 cm (1/4 inch) Cut into approximately 30 biscuits with a 5 cm (2 inch) fluted biscuit cutter. Cook in the centre of the oven for 12–15 minutes. Allow the biscuits to cool on the baking trays for 5 minutes before transferring them to a wire rack. Store in an airtight container when cold.

Coconut Macaroons

ingredients

2 egg whites
Pinch of salt
150 g (5 oz) caster sugar
150 g (5 oz) desiccated coconut
Rice paper
10 glacé cherries, halved

makes

20 macaroons

Preheat the oven to 160°C. In a bowl, whisk the egg whites with the salt, adding the sugar, a little at a time, until the mixture is stiff and forming peaks. Gently fold in the coconut. Line a baking tray with rice paper and put 20 well spaced spoonfuls of the mixture onto the paper. Top each with half a glacé cherry. Bake for 25–30 minutes until firm, cool on the rice paper. Tear or cut the paper around each macaroon when cool.

Crispy Coconut Biscuits with Coconut Rum Cream

ingredients

120 g (4 oz) butter
240 g (8 oz) caster sugar
1 egg
300 g (10 oz) self-raising flour
Pinch of salt
90 g (3 oz) desiccated coconut

coconut cream

180 g (6 oz) icing sugar
30 g (1 oz) softened butter
2–3 tbsp desiccated coconut
2 tbsp coconut flavoured rum

makes

About 30 biscuits

Preheat the oven to 180°C. Cream the butter with 210 g (7 oz) of the sugar, in a bowl. Beat in the egg, sieved flour, salt and coconut. Roll the mixture into balls. Flatten the balls, then coat the top and sides in the remaining caster sugar before baking on silicone paper for 10–15 minutes, or until crisp.

To make the coconut cream: combine the icing sugar with the butter in a bowl. Beat until smooth then add the desiccated coconut and rum. Continue beating, adding extra icing sugar if required. Sandwich the biscuits together with coconut cream. Store in an airtight container.

Crunchy Walnut and Cornflake Drops

ingredients

180 g (6 oz) butter
1 tsp vanilla essence
60 g (2 oz) sugar
2 eggs
270 g (9 oz) self-raising flour
Pinch of bicarbonate soda
2 tbsp single cream
60 g (2 oz) ready to eat dried
 apricots, chopped
60 g (2 oz) sultanas
60 g (2 oz) glacé cherries, chopped
90 g (3 oz) crushed walnuts
90 g (3 oz) lightly crushed cornflakes

makes

Approximately 30 biscuits

Preheat the oven to 180°C. Cream together the butter, vanilla essence and sugar in a bowl until nearly white. Beat in the eggs one at a time.

Sift together the flour and bicarbonate of soda, then fold one-third into the creamed mix. Add one tablespoon of cream, gently fold in another third of the flour mix, followed by the other tablespoon of cream. Gently mix in the remaining flour, then stir in the apricots, sultanas and glacé cherries.

Mix the crushed walnuts and cornflakes together in a flat dish. Divide the wet mixture into tablespoon-sized balls and place into the cornflake and nut mix. Press the balls until flattened and coated. Place on silicone paper leaving space for the biscuits to spread.

Bake for approximately 15 minutes, or until crisp and golden. Transfer to a wire rack to cool. Store in an airtight container

Peanut Crunchies

ingredients

120 g (4 oz) almond marzipan
90 g (3 oz) peanut butter
240 g (8 oz) marshmallows
60 g (2 oz) plain chocolate
180 g (6 oz) sugar coated cornflakes

makes

20 biscuits

Place the marzipan, peanut butter, marshmallows and chocolate in a saucepan and gently melt over a low heat, stirring constantly. Add the cornflakes and mix well. Press the mixture into a lined 20 cm (8 inch) square tin and allow to cool. Cut into 20 bars when set. Store in an airtight container.

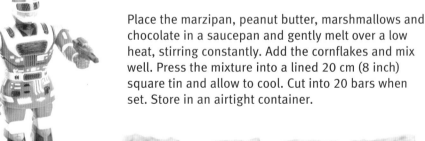

Marshmallow Cornflake Drops

ingredients
60 g (2 oz) butter
240 g (8 oz) marshmallows
180 g (6 oz) cornflakes

makes
Approximately 25 biscuits

Melt the butter and marshmallows in a pan over a low heat stirring until melted. Remove from the heat and add the cornflakes, mixing well with a moistened spoon. Shape into small balls and place on silicone paper, until cool and firm. Store in an airtight container.

Coffee and Almond Crunch Biscuits

ingredients

120 g (4 oz) butter
90 g (3 oz) sugar
90 g (3 oz) ground almonds
Pinch of salt
1 tsp lemon juice
195 g (6 $1/2$ oz) plain flour

coffee icing

270 g (9 oz) icing sugar
1 tbsp softened butter
1 $1/2$ tbsp instant coffee granules
$1/2$ tbsp hot water
1 tbsp brandy
30 whole almonds, lightly toasted

makes

30 biscuits

Preheat the oven to 180°C. Cream the butter and sugar in a bowl, then beat in the ground almonds, salt and lemon juice. Stir in the sieved flour to make a firm dough. Carefully roll out the dough until approximately 3 mm thick. Cut out 30 cookie rounds using a 6 cm (2 $1/2$ inch) fluted cutter. Bake on a tray with greased silicone paper until golden and crisp. Cool on wire racks.

To make the icing: sift the icing sugar into a small basin and add the butter. Dissolve the coffee granules in the hot water and add, along with the brandy, to the icing. Beat all the ingredients together until the mixture is smooth. Carefully spread the icing over the biscuits keeping the edges neat. Decorate with a single almond on each one. Store in an airtight container.

Orange, Lemon and Lime Crunchies

ingredients

120 g (4 oz) butter
90 g (3 oz) caster sugar
Grated rind of $1/2$ orange
Juice and zest of $1/2$ lemon
1 tsp lime juice
45 g ($1^1/2$ oz) ground walnuts
150 g (5 oz) self-raising flour
30 g (1 oz) crushed walnuts

makes

30 biscuits

Preheat the oven to 190°C. Cream the butter and 60g (2oz) of the sugar in a bowl, then add the orange rind, lemon juice and zest, lime juice and ground walnuts. Beat in the sieved flour until the mixture begins to hold together.

Divide the dough into 30 small balls. Drop each one into the crushed walnuts and remaining sugar. Flatten each ball slightly and place on greased silicone paper on a baking tray.

Bake for 10–12 minutes, until golden. Allow to cool, then transfer to wire racks. Store in an airtight container.

65

ingredients

120 g (4 oz) butter
90 g (3 oz) icing sugar
1 tsp lemon juice
150 g (5 oz) self-raising flour
75 g (2 1/2 oz) cornflour
2 tsp grated lemon zest
1 egg yolk
2 tsp milk
Extra icing sugar

filling

60 g (2 oz) cream cheese
2 tbsp cottage cheese
2 tbsp sugar
1/2 tsp grated lemon zest
1 tbsp coconut flavoured rum
2 tbsp desiccated coconut
1 egg yolk

makes

25–30 biscuits

Lemon and Coconut Biscuits

Cream the butter, icing sugar and lemon juice in a bowl until light and fluffy. Add the sieved flours and lemon zest and mix to form a dough. Knead the dough until smooth, wrap in cling film and refrigerate until firm.

Roll out the dough out on a floured surface until 3 mm thick. Use a fluted cutter to cut into 6 cm (2$^1/2$ inch) rounds. Place half the biscuits on greased silicone paper and brush the edges with a little egg yolk.

To make the filling: beat the cream cheese, cottage cheese, sugar, lemon zest, coconut flavoured rum and coconut together in a bowl. Mix in the egg yolk and store the mixture in the fridge for 20 minutes.

Place half a teaspoon of filling in the centre of each biscuit and place another biscuit on top. Gently press together to seal the edges. Brush the

tops with egg wash, made from the remaining egg yolk and a little milk. Bake for 12–15 minutes, until golden brown. Cool on wire racks then dust with icing sugar. Store in an airtight container.

White Chocolate and Exotic Fruit Cookies

ingredients

210 g (7 oz) plain flour
1 tsp baking powder
105 g (3 ½ oz) unsalted butter
135 g (4 ½ oz) light brown sugar
75 g (2 ½ oz) white chocolate, chopped
75 g (2 ½ oz) of mixed exotic dried fruit (papaya, pineapple etc) mango, chopped
1 tsp lemon zest
1 egg

makes

Approximately 18 cookies

Preheat the oven to 190°C. Line two baking trays with lightly greased baking parchment. Sift the flour and baking powder into a bowl. Rub the butter into the flour with your fingertips. Mix in the sugar, chopped chocolate and dried fruit. Add the lemon zest and egg, plus a little extra water if necessary, to form a soft dough.

Place spoonfuls of the mixture on the baking trays, pressing each mound down slightly with the back of a spoon. Cook for 10–12 minutes until light, golden brown. Allow to cool for 5 minutes, then transfer to a wire rack. Store in an airtight container.

Ginger Nuts with Sticky Ginger Centres

ingredients

360 g (12 oz) self-raising flour
Pinch of salt
1 tbsp ground ginger
210 g (7 oz) caster sugar
1 tsp bicarbonate of soda
90 g (3 oz) golden syrup
135 g (4 1/2 oz) butter
1 beaten egg
1 tsp grated lemon zest
1 1/2 tbsp stem ginger, chopped

makes

25–30 biscuits

Preheat the oven to 160°C. Sift the flour, salt, ground ginger, caster sugar and bicarbonate of soda into a large bowl. Gently heat 70 g (2 1/2 oz) of the golden syrup and the butter together in a small pan until the butter has melted. Allow mixture to cool slightly before pouring into the dry ingredients. Add the egg and lemon zest and mix to a firm dough. Divide the mixture into 25–30 balls.

Mix the finely chopped stem ginger with remaining golden syrup and add a little extra ground ginger to stiffen the mixture. Take the balls of cookie dough and make a depression in the centre with a finger. Place half a teaspoon of ginger mix in the centre of the ball and bring over the sides to seal in the ginger. Place the cookies, sealed side down, on lightly greased silicone paper on a baking tray and press gently to flatten. Bake for 15–20 minutes until a pale golden colour then transfer onto a wire rack to cool. This will leave the biscuits slightly soft with sticky centres. For crisper biscuits cook a little longer. Store in an airtight container.

Brandy Snaps

ingredients

120 g (4 oz) butter
120 g (4 oz) golden syrup
120 g (4 oz) demerara sugar
1 1/2 tsp ground ginger
120 g (4 oz) plain flour
1 tsp lemon juice

makes

25–30 brandy snaps

Preheat the oven to 180°C. Melt the butter in a pan with the golden syrup and sugar. Allow to cool slightly and mix in the ginger followed by the sieved flour and lemon juice. Blend well and drop heaped teaspoonfuls of the mixture onto greased baking trays. Allowing space around each biscuit for spreading, spread the spoonfuls out gently.

Cook for a few minutes until golden brown and leave on the trays until the brandy snaps are cool enough to handle. Lift each one with a palette knife and roll quickly around the handle of a wooden spoon, keeping them loose enough to remove when cold. Make a few at a time, as the biscuits will only roll while they are warm (although a few moments back in the oven will soften set biscuits enough for shaping). Store on layers of cling film, in an airtight container.

Hazelnut and Pink Grapefruit Cookies

ingredients
140 g (5 oz) plain flour
2 tbsp sugar
90 g (3 oz) ground hazelnuts
110 g (4 oz) butter
1 egg yolk
1 tsp grated pink grapefruit zest
1 1/2 tbsp pink grapefruit juice
50 ml double cream, whipped
30 whole hazelnuts
Orange zest

filling
60 g (2 oz) butter
120 g (4 oz) sugar
2 tsp grated, grapefruit zest
2 tbsp grapefruit juice
2 eggs

makes
30 biscuits

Preheat the oven to 180°C. Sift the flour and mix with the sugar and hazelnuts. Rub in the butter and add the egg yolk, pink grapefruit zest and juice, mixing to form a smooth dough. Divide the dough into two, press one half into a lined and greased baking tin, approximately 15 x 30 cm (6 x 12 inches) and 1 cm (1/2 inch) deep. Refrigerate both whilst preparing the filling.

Begin the filling by creaming the butter and sugar. Beat in the pink grapefruit zest and juice and then the eggs. The mixture will appear curdled, but this is normal. Spread this mixture over the refrigerated base, and, using the coarse side of a grater, grate the remaining half of the dough over the mixture. Bake for about 30 minutes or until pale, golden brown. Cool on wire racks (during cooling the layers often merge together). Cut into fingers once completely cold.

Decorate by piping a noisette of whipped cream in the centre of each cookie and top with hazelnuts and strands of orange zest.

Hazelnut and Sesame Fingers

ingredients

180 g (6 oz) ground hazelnuts
60 g (2 oz) ground almonds
120 g (4 oz) sesame seeds
45 g (1^1/$_2$ oz) plain flour
3 egg whites
180 g (6 oz) caster sugar
180 g (6 oz) dark chocolate

makes
25–30 biscuits

Preheat the oven to 160°C. Combine the hazelnuts, almonds, sesame seeds and sieved flour in a bowl and mix well. Place the egg whites in a clean bowl and beat with an electric mixer until stiff. Add sugar and beat until really stiff and velvety.

Fold in the nut mixture, then transfer into a piping tool or bag with a large plain tube or nozzle. Pipe fingers of the mixture onto lightly greased silicone paper on baking trays and bake for 12–15 minutes until crisp and golden. Leave to cool.

Melt the chocolate in a bowl over a pan of simmering water, then dip in one end of each biscuit. Allow the chocolate on the biscuits to set. Store biscuits in an airtight container.

Honey and Ginger Snaps

ingredients

60 g (2 oz) butter
2 tbsp clear honey
1 tbsp demerara sugar
30 g (1 oz) stem ginger,
  finely chopped
90 g (3 oz) flaked almonds
120 g (4 oz) cornflakes

makes

25–30 biscuits

Preheat the oven to 180°C. Over a gentle heat, melt the butter with the honey and sugar. Mix together the stem ginger, flaked almonds and cornflakes in a bowl. Pour the butter and honey mixture over the top and gently mix until the cornflakes are evenly coated. Spoon the mixture into small paper cases and bake in the oven for 8–10 minutes. Allow to cool until firm. Store in an airtight container.

Honey Flapjacks with Pecans and Almonds

ingredients

210 g (7 oz) butter
3 tbsp clear honey
210 g (7 oz) demerara sugar
285 g (9^1/$_2$ oz) jumbo rolled oats
105 g (3^1/$_2$ oz) desiccated coconut
45 g (1^1/$_2$oz) flaked almonds
45 g (1^1/$_2$oz) pecans, lightly crushed

makes

25–30 biscuits

Preheat the oven to 170°C. Gently heat the butter, honey and demerara sugar in a large saucepan until just melted. Stir in the oats, coconut, flaked almonds and pecan nuts, and mix well. Spread the mixture evenly in a well oiled 20 cm (8 inch) square baking tray. Bake in the oven for approximately 30 minutes. Allow to cool in the tray for 10–12 minutes then cut into squares with a sharp knife. Transfer the flapjacks to a wire rack to cool completely. Store in an airtight container.

Chocolate-dipped Meringues with Rum and Crystallised Pineapple

ingredients

2 egg whites
120 g (4 oz) caster sugar
120 g (4 oz) dark chocolate
30 g (1 oz) icing sugar
$1/2$ pint double cream
2 tbsp rum
45 g ($1^1/2$ oz) crystallised pineapple

makes

25–30 biscuits

Preheat the oven to its lowest setting. Using an electric whisk, beat the egg whites in a bowl, until they form stiff peaks. Add half the caster sugar and beat until glossy. Gently fold in the remaining sugar. Fill a piping tool or bag with meringue mix and, using a large, plain nozzle, pipe small circles onto greased silicone paper on a baking sheet. Place in the oven and cook for 2–3 hours. Turn the heat off and leave the meringues in the oven overnight to crisp.

Melt the chocolate in a bowl over a pan of simmering water. Dip the base of each meringue in chocolate. Place them on wax paper until the chocolate has set.

Add the icing sugar to the double cream and beat until nearly stiff. Add the rum and beat to piping consistency. Pipe a nest of rum flavoured cream on each meringue and fill the centre with chopped crystallised pineapple. Drizzle any remaining chocolate over the top. Best served within 2–3 hours.

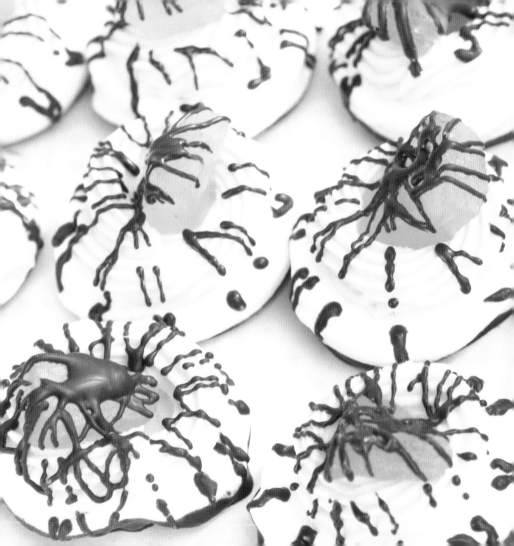

Chocolate and Orange Liqueur Meringue Kisses

ingredients

4 egg whites
Pinch of salt
270 g (9 oz) caster sugar
60 g (2 oz) dark chocolate
1/2 pint double cream
2–3 tbsp of orange liqueur

makes

About 20 meringues

Preheat the oven to 120°C. In a clean bowl, use an electric whisk to beat the egg whites and salt until stiff – you should be able to turn the bowl upside down. Gradually whisk in the caster sugar a little at a time until it has all been incorporated and the meringue mixture is thick and glossy and will stand in stiff peaks.

Transfer the mixture to a piping tube with a medium-sized nozzle. Pipe small, even rosettes onto a baking sheet covered with silicone paper. Bake for one-and-a-half hours without colouring the meringues. When they can be lifted off the paper cleanly, turn off the oven but leave the meringues inside overnight to crisp.

Melt the chocolate over a pan of simmering water and dip in the bases of the crisp meringues. leave to set on a sheet of silicone paper.

Whisk the double cream with a little extra caster sugar. When beaten, mix in the orange liqueur and continue to beat until it reaches piping consistency. Sandwich the meringues together with the cream mixture just before they are served.

Cereal Crisps

ingredients

120 g (4 oz) butter
180 g (6 oz) caster sugar
1 egg
120 g (4 oz) self-raising flour
30 g (1 oz) plain flour
45 g (1 1/2 oz) rolled oats
45 g (1 1/2 oz) sesame seeds
45 g (1 1/2 oz) flaked almonds,
   lightly crushed
45 g (1 1/2 oz) cornflakes

makes

25–30 biscuits

Preheat the oven to 180°C. Cream the butter and sugar until light and fluffy in a bowl. Beat the egg then add it to the mixture. Fold in the sieved flours, oats, seeds, nuts and cornflakes, and mix well. Place tablespoons of mixture onto lightly oiled silicone paper on a baking tray; press flat and bake for 15 minutes or until golden and crisp. Store in an airtight container.

Oat Crunch Cookies

ingredients

120 g (4 oz) butter
90 g (3 oz) demerara sugar
120 g (4 oz) plain wholemeal flour
120 g (4 oz) porridge oats

makes

Approximately 25 cookies

Preheat the oven to 180°C. Cream the butter and sugar together in a bowl, until light. Add the sieved flour and oats to the mixture and use your hands to create a soft dough. Roll the dough out on a floured surface until 5 mm thick and cut into 25 rounds with a 5 cm (2 inch) cutter. Bake in the oven for 12–15 minutes or until cooked. Transfer to a wire rack to cool. Store in an airtight container.

Chocolate Chip and Peanut Cookies

ingredients

135 g (4 ½ oz) unsalted butter,
  softened
45 g (1 ½oz) smooth
  peanut butter
75 g (2 ½ oz) sugar
2 large eggs
1 tsp vanilla essence
210 g (7 oz) plain flour
1 tsp baking powder
75 g (2 ½ oz) dark chocolate,
  chopped
45 g (1 ½ oz) unsalted peanuts

makes

Approximately 18 cookies

powder together and fold them
into the mixture. Add the chopped
chocolate and peanuts. Mix in
1–2 tablespoonfuls of milk if the
dough appears too stiff.

Preheat the oven to 180°. Line a
baking tray with silicone paper. Beat
the butter, peanut butter and sugar
in a bowl, until fluffy. Add the beaten
eggs and vanilla essence, and mix
well. Sift the flour and baking

Place evenly spaced spoonfuls of
the mixture onto the baking tray,
pressing each one down with the
back of the spoon. (Dipping the
spoon in water will stop it sticking to
the dough.) Bake cookies in the
centre of the oven for 20 minutes.
Allow them to cool on a wire rack.
Store in an airtight container.

Crunchy Peanut and Orange Squash Cookies

ingredients

120 g (4 oz) self-raising flour
$^1/_2$ tsp cinnamon
$^1/_2$ tsp bicarbonate of soda
30 g (1 oz) rolled oats
180 g (6 oz) caster sugar
30 g (1 oz) desiccated coconut
1 tsp finely grated orange zest
120 g (4 oz) crunchy peanut butter
1 tbsp golden syrup
2 tbsp orange squash
1 tbsp orange juice

makes
23–30 biscuits

Preheat the oven to 180˚C. Sift the flour, cinnamon and bicarbonate of soda into a bowl and stir in the rolled oats, caster sugar, coconut and orange zest. Rub the peanut butter into the mixture until it resembles coarse breadcrumbs.

Make a well in the centre and add the golden syrup and orange squash to make a soft dough, adding a little orange juice, if necessary. Remove the dough from the bowl and knead until smooth. Wrap in cling film and refrigerate until firm.

When ready to use, roll out the dough on a floured surface until approximately 1 cm ($^1/_2$ inch) thick. Using a 5 cm (2$^1/_2$ inch) fluted cutter, cut into biscuit rounds. Place on greased silicone paper on a baking sheet and cook for 8–10 minutes until pale, golden brown. Cool on a wire rack and store in an airtight container.

Peanut and Shortbread Caramel Cookies

ingredients

105 g (3 1/2 oz) plain flour
45 g (1 1/2 oz) self-raising flour
90 g (3 oz) butter
1 egg

topping

90 g (3 oz) butter
120 g (4 oz) demerara sugar
1 tbsp golden syrup
120 g (4 oz) roasted
  unsalted peanuts

makes

32 small biscuits

Preheat the oven to 180°C. Sift the flours into a bowl and rub in the butter. Beat the egg and add to the mixture to create a firm dough. Press the dough into a lined baking tray 30 x 15 cm (12 x 6 inch) and 3 cm (1 1/4 inch) deep. Smooth the mixture by pressing down with a palette knife and bake for 15 minutes.

To make the topping, melt the butter, demerara sugar and golden syrup in a small saucepan. Simmer gently for 5 minutes. Remove from the heat and stir in the nuts. Pour the mixture over the base in the baking tray and return it to the oven for a further 5 minutes. Allow to cool in the tin then cut into small squares.

Peanut Butter Crunchies

ingredients

120 g (4 oz) butter
45 g (1 1/2 oz) caster sugar
45 g (1 1/2 oz) demerara sugar
Pinch of salt
1/2 tsp vanilla essence
90 g (3 oz) peanut butter
1/2 tsp grated lemon zest
1 tsp bicarbonate of soda
30 g (1 oz) crushed peanuts
180 g (6 oz) plain flour

makes

25–30 biscuits

Preheat the oven to 180°C. Cream the butter, sugars and salt together in a bowl. Beat in the vanilla essence, peanut butter and grated lemon zest. Fold in the bicarbonate of soda, crushed peanuts and the sieved flour, to form a stiff dough. Roll dough into small balls and place on greased baking sheets. Use a knife to press down the biscuits and bake for 12–15 minutes until crisp and golden. When cold, store in an airtight container.

Pecan and Coffee Squares

ingredients
120 g (4 oz) butter
60 g (2 oz) caster sugar
150 g (5 oz) plain flour
45 g (1 1/2 oz) self-raising flour

filling
420 g (14 oz) condensed milk
2 tbsp golden syrup
30 g (1 oz) butter
3 tsp instant coffee granules
90 g (3 oz) crushed pecan nuts

topping
150 g (5 oz) plain flour
1 tsp cinnamon
1 tsp instant coffee powder
60 g (2 oz) brown sugar
120 g (4 oz) butter

makes
28 biscuits

Preheat the oven to 180°C. Cream the butter and sugar in a bowl, before adding the sieved flours to make a firm dough. Press into the base of a well-greased 25–30 cm (10–12 inch) swiss roll tin and bake for 10–12 minutes.

To make the filling: mix the condensed milk, golden syrup and butter together in a non-stick saucepan. Add the coffee granules, then heat the mixture over a medium heat until it starts to bubble. Stir briskly until it thickens, but do not allow to burn. Mix in the pecans.

To make the topping: sift the dry ingredients into a bowl and rub in the butter to make a firm dough. Chill in the refrigerator until very firm.

Spread the filling over the biscuit base, then coarsely grate the topping over the top. Return to the oven and cook for a further 10–12 minutes, or until firm to the touch. Allow to cool before cutting into squares.

Pecan and Honey Slices

ingredients

120 g (4 oz) butter
120 g (4 oz) caster sugar
1 egg yolk
150 g (5 oz) plain flour
45 g (1 1/2 oz) self-raising flour
2 tbsp custard powder
1/2 tsp salt

topping

120 g (4 oz) demerara sugar
1 tbsp clear honey
90 g (3 oz) butter
120 g (2 oz) crushed pecans
120 g (2 oz) walnut pieces

makes

24 biscuits

Preheat the oven to 180°C. Cream the butter and sugar together in a bowl, until fluffy. Beat in the egg yolk then mix in the sieved flours, custard powder and salt. Mix to a firm dough and press into a swiss roll tin measuring 15 x 30 cm (6 x 12 inches). Bake for 15 minutes until golden brown.

To make the topping: place the sugar, honey and butter in a small saucepan and melt over a low heat. Simmer gently for 3–4 minutes and then stir in the crushed pecans and walnuts. Spread with the topping mixture over the biscuit base. Return to the oven and bake for 5 minutes. Allow to cool in the tin, then cut into rectangles.

Traditional Shortbread Wheel

ingredients

240 g (8 oz) butter
300 g (10 oz) plain flour
2 tbsp ground rice
60 g (2 oz) icing sugar

makes

24 biscuits
2 'wheels' of shortbread

Preheat the oven to 160°C. Rub the butter into the sieved flour, ground rice and icing sugar. Bring the dough together and press into two greased, 17 cm (7 inch) cake tins. Use your finger to crimp around the edges and prick the surface with a fork to prevent the mixture rising. Score the surface of each wheel into 12 segments with the back of a knife.

Bake in the oven for 35–40 minutes, until a pale golden brown. Leave to stand in the tins for 10–15 minutes then lift out onto a wire rack to cool. This mixture can also be used to press into the traditional carved, wooden mould which produces ornately patterned shortbread biscuits. Store in an airtight container.

Piped Butter Shortbread

ingredients

240 g (8 oz) butter
225 g (7 1/2 oz) plain flour
90 g (3 oz) icing sugar
2 tsp grated lemon zest
Icing sugar to decorate

makes

Approximately 23–30 biscuits

Preheat the oven to 180°C. Have all the ingredients at room temperature to assist mixing. Combine the butter with the sieved flour, icing sugar and lemon zest. Use an electric mixer at low speed to beat the ingredients for 10 minutes.

Spoon the mixture into a piping tool or bag and, using a large, star-shaped nozzle, pipe 6 cm (2 1/2 inches) sticks, piping two or three sticks together to form each biscuit onto a greased baking sheet. Bake for 10–15 minutes, or until golden. Leave on the tray until nearly cool then transfer to wire racks. Dust with icing sugar before serving. Store in an airtight container.

Piped Viennese Shortbread with White Chocolate and Pistachios

ingredients
240 g (8 oz) butter
60 g (2 oz) caster sugar
1/2 tsp vanilla essence
270 g (9 oz) plain flour
45 g (1 1/2 oz) rice flour
Pinch of salt
120 g (4 oz) white chocolate, melted
30 g (1 oz) chopped pistachio nuts

makes
Approximately 25–30 biscuits

Preheat the oven to 180°C. Cream the butter and sugar in a bowl, until light and fluffy. Add the vanilla essence and fold in the sieved flours and salt. Spoon into a piping bag and, using a large star nozzle, pipe biscuits onto lightly greased silicone paper.

Bake for 10–12 minutes until golden brown. When cold, dip one end into the melted chocolate and sprinkle with pistachio nuts. Store in an airtight container.

Piped Rich Shortbread with Dark Chocolate Chips and Stem Ginger

ingredients

240 g (8 oz) butter
4 tbsp icing sugar
1 tsp vanilla essence
120 g (4 oz) plain flour
150 g (5 oz) cornflour
30 g (1 oz) dark chocolate chips
30 g (1 oz) stem ginger, finely diced

makes

16 cookies

Preheat the oven to 180°C. Cream the butter with the sieved icing sugar in a bowl, and whisk until light and fluffy. Beat in the vanilla essence, sieved plain flour and cornflour until smooth. Place the mixture in a piping bag and, with a large star nozzle, pipe 6 cm (2^1/$_2$ inch) biscuits onto greased silicone paper on a baking sheet.

Sprinkle a few dark chocolate chips and a little stem ginger down the centre of each biscuit and bake in the oven for 10–12 minutes until pale, golden brown. Cool on a wire rack. Store in an airtight container.

Chocolate Fudge Brownies

ingredients
2 eggs
240 g (8 oz) caster sugar
105 g (3 1/2 oz) butter
3 tbsp cocoa powder
105 g (3 1/2 oz) self-raising flour
45 g (1 1/2 oz) pecans, chopped

fudge icing
45 g (1 1/2 oz) butter
1 tbsp milk
105 g (3 1/2 oz) icing sugar
2 tbsp cocoa powder
Pecan or walnut halves, to decorate

makes
15 brownies

Preheat the oven to 180°C. Beat the eggs and the sugar together in a bowl, until light and fluffy. Melt the butter and beat in the cocoa powder before adding to the eggs and sugar. Sift the flour and fold into the main mix with the pecans. Pour into a lined, greased 20 cm (8 inch) square cake tin. Bake for 40–45 minutes.

To make the fudge icing: melt the butter and add the milk. Remove from the heat then beat in the icing sugar and cocoa powder. Spread icing over the cooked brownie and decorate with pecans or walnut halves. Cut into squares when the topping is firm.

Sticky Chocolate and Orange Liqueur Brownies

ingredients

105 g (3 1/2 oz) unsalted butter
180 g (6 oz) caster sugar
75 g (2 1/2 oz) demerara sugar
135 g (4 1/2 oz) dark chocolate
1 tbsp dark treacle
2 eggs
1 tsp grated orange zest
2 tbsp orange liqueur
105 g (3 1/2 oz) plain flour
2 1/2 tbsp cocoa powder
1/2 tsp baking powder

makes

20 brownies

until light. Beat in the chocolate mixture and fold in the sieved flour, cocoa powder and baking powder.

Using a metal spoon, spoon the mixture into a lined and greased 20 cm (8 inch) square cake tin. Bake for 25 minutes. The mixture will begin to shrink and the top will be crisp although the middle will still be soft. Allow the cake to cool in the tin then cut into rectangles. Store in an airtight container.

the oven to 180°C. Melt the
rs. dark chocolate
a low heat.
allow to cool.
e zest and
er in a bowl,

Chocolate Liqueur Cups

ingredients

120 g (4 oz) dark chocolate
1 packet of 2.5 cm (1 inch)
  silver foil cases

filling

1 egg yolk
60 g (2 oz) icing sugar
60 g (2 oz) butter
120 g (4 oz) dark chocolate
1 tsp coffee granules
1 tsp hot water
1 tsp coffee liqueur
Any of the following to decorate:
  toasted whole almonds, hazelnuts,
  pecans, glacé pineapple

makes

20 liqueur cups

Melt the chocolate in a clean bowl over a pan of simmering water and place one teaspoonful in each foil case. Using a pastry brush, draw the chocolate up the sides of the case until the inside is well coated, leave to set.

To make the filling: place the egg yolk and icing sugar in a bowl and whisk together over a pan of water on a gentle heat. When thick, allow to cool then beat in the butter. Melt the chocolate and mix into the filling a little at a time.

Dissolve the coffee granules in the hot water, mix with the coffee liqueur and pour into the main mix. Continue to beat the mixture until thick. Transfer to a piping bag and, using a medium star piping nozzle, fill the chocolate cases. Use nuts and glacé fruit to decorate. Leave to harden, then peel away the foil cases when set.

Chocolate Cups with Fruit and Nuts

ingredients

105 g (3 ½ oz) dark chocolate
Paper sweet cases

filling

210 g (7 oz) mascarpone cheese
½ tsp of your favourite liqueur
A mixture of the following: black
   or white grapes, fresh raspberries,
   strawberries, almonds,
   hazelnuts, macadamia nuts
105 g (3½ oz) milk chocolate

makes

20 chocolate cups

Melt the dark chocolate in a clean bowl over a pan of simmering water. Place approximately one teaspoon of chocolate in each paper case. Using a pastry brush, draw the chocolate up the sides of the mould until it is well coated, leave to cool.

To make the filling: mix the mascarpone cheese, your chosen liqueur and the fruit and nuts together in a bowl. Melt the milk chocolate in a bowl over a pan of simmering water, beat into the cheese filling a little at a time. Place the mixture in a piping tool and, using medium star nozzle, fill the paper cases. Use any remaining nuts or pieces of fruit to decorate.

Chocolate Fudge Squares with Brazil Nuts and Sultanas

ingredients

270 g (9 oz) dark chocolate
30 g (1 oz) peanut butter
4 tbsp evaporated milk
480 g (1 lb) icing sugar
45 g (1¹/₂ oz) Brazil nuts
30 g (1 oz) pistachio nuts, chopped
45 g (1¹/₂ oz) sultanas
Paper sweet cases

makes

64 fudge squares

Finely chop the chocolate and place in a bowl over a pan of hot water. Add the peanut butter and evaporated milk and stir until all the ingredients are well combined. Remove from the heat and beat in the icing sugar a little at a time. Chop the Brazil nuts and fold them into the chocolate mix along with the pistachio nuts and sultanas.

Pour into in a well-greased 20 cm (8 inch) tin and gently press to smooth the top. Refrigerate until very firm, turn out onto a board and cut into small squares. Place each square in a paper sweet case and chill for an hour.

Almond and Walnut Crunchies

ingredients

180 g (6 oz) blanched almonds
2 egg whites
120 g (4 oz) caster sugar
1 tsp finely grated orange zest
2 tbsp orange liqueur
60 g (2 oz) crushed walnuts
26 walnut halves

makes

26 biscuits

Preheat the oven to 190°C. Finely chop the blanched almonds in a food processor. Add one egg white, sugar, orange zest and orange liqueur to the almonds and mix until combined. Roll out the dough on a lightly floured surface until approximately 1 cm (1/2 inch) thick, then cut out 26 biscuits using a 5 cm (2 inch) cutter. Place biscuits on a greased baking sheet.

Toast the crushed walnuts in the oven for 3–4 minutes then finely crush them with a rolling pin. Brush the tops of the biscuits with unbeaten egg white and press into the crushed walnuts. Dip the walnut halves into the egg white and press them into the centre of each biscuit. Bake for 5–10 minutes until golden. Cook on wire racks and store in an airtight container.

Caramel and Dark Chocolate Walnut Slices

ingredients

75 g (2 1/2 oz) self-raising flour
60 g (2 oz) caster sugar
120 g (4 oz) desiccated coconut
30 g (1 oz) cocoa powder
60 g (2 oz) butter

Topping

2 eggs
240 g (8 oz) demerara sugar
1 tsp vanilla essence
120 g (4 oz) desiccated coconut
1/2 tsp baking powder
90 g (3 oz) crushed walnuts
120 g (4 oz) dark chocolate

makes

24 biscuits

Preheat the oven to 180°C. To make the base, mix the sieved flour, caster sugar, coconut and cocoa powder together in a bowl. Melt the butter and beat into the dry mixture to form a dough. Transfer to a swiss roll tin 15 x 30 cm (6 x 12 inch) and use a palette knife to press the dough out evenly. Bake for 15 minutes.

To make the topping: beat the eggs with the demerara sugar and vanilla essence in a bowl. Mix in the coconut, baking powder and crushed walnuts and beat. Spread the mixture over the partially cooked base; return it to the oven and cook for 20 minutes until the topping is golden. Cut into rectangles and dip the bases into some melted dark chocolate. Leave to set, then store in an airtight container.

Technical Terms

The following list will be a useful source of reference for technical terms used, not only in this book, but in recipes featured in other cookery books or on the internet.

Absorb – for one ingredient to take in another

Almond paste – a mixture of ground almonds and sugar

Bake blind – to bake flans or tarts unfilled for filling at a later stage

Baking – to cook in an oven at a pre-set temperature

Baking parchment – non-stick paper prepared especially for cooking on, also know as silicone paper

Baking sheet – a flat, metal tray on which cakes and biscuits can be baked

Beat – to aerate or mix ingredients using a spoon or whisk

Blanche – to remove the skins of nuts by immersing them in boiling water

Cake tin – metal shaped tin in which cakes and biscuits can be cooked

Candied – preservation by cooking or immersing in sugar

Celsius – temperature scale where 0° equals the freezing point of water and 100° is the boiling point of water

Coat – to cover one ingredient with another. Coat in chocolate, icing or a sauce, for example

Cream – to beat ingredients together until light and fluffy, the mixture should be nearly white. Or, a dairy product made from the skimmed fat content of fresh milk

Cream of tartar – one of the components of baking powder

Crimping – to make a decorative edge, for example around the edge of a pie or shortbread

Cutters – shaped metal or plastic tool used to cut rolled doughs to a required shape

Dilute – to add a liquid to reduce the strength of a mixture

Docher – to pierce holes with a fork or a spiked implement in order to prevent rising

Dough – a mixture of flour, water and often fat. A firm, thick and uncooked mixture

Drain – to strain solids from liquids using a colander or strainer

Dust – sprinkle flour or icing sugar over tables and boards to prevent dough sticking

Egg wash – a mixture of beaten egg and milk or water, used to glaze baked foods

Essence – a flavouring agent

Essential oils – as above, but extracted from fruits and nuts, and used to strengthen flavours

Technical Terms

Fahrenheit – temperature scale where 32° represents the freezing point of water and 212° equals the boiling point of water

Flaked – to cut into thin slices, sometimes called slivered, as in nuts or almonds

Fold – to mix with other ingredients by gently turning one part over the other with a spoon

Glaze – to make something shine by either coating with a shiny mix, such as boiled jams, or to caramelise the sugars using an intense heat

Grease – to cover the inside of a cake or baking tray with fat

Hard flour – flour which contains a high proportion of gluten, sometimes called strong bread flour

Icing sugar – finely powdered white sugar

Knead – to mix together by working with the hands

Line – to cover the inside of a baking tray or tin with paper

Liqueurs – strongly flavoured spirits, usually sweetened

Marzipan – a cooked almond and sugar paste used for cakes and biscuits

Nibs or Nibbed – usually almonds or nuts broken into small squares

Piping – to force a mixture through a bag or piping tool to produce a decorative shape

Technical Terms

Puff pastry – a pastry produced by laminating layers of dough and fat

Rice flour – finely ground rice used in shortbreads and macaroons, either to save on almonds or to add texture to the surface of the mix

Rub-in – to work fat and flour together, usually by hand, to produce a crumb-like texture

Shredded – to cut into very fine strips

Sieve – a wire mesh which removes lumps from liquids or dry mixtures

Silicone paper – also known as baking parchment, this is a heat resistant paper that reduces sticking during cooking

Sodium bicarbonate – alpha component of baking powder which produces carbon dioxide to aerate a mixture

Soft flour – flour with very little gluten content

Strong flour – as hard flour

Wafer paper – usually referred to as rice paper, edible paper used for macaroons

Whip – to beat with a whisk to trap air and thicken

Yield – the amount any recipe will produce

Zest – the outside rind of citrus fruit which is often grated and used as a flavouring agent

Conclusion

Most of us lead busy lives and it may be tempting to pick up a packet of cookies from the supermarket shelf, but the ease and convenience of buying cookies is surpassed by the sheer pleasure derived from baking your own. There is an almost sensual delight in the fusion of sweet and aromatic ingredients as they fuse together to produce the tastes and smells of home baking.

Many exciting textures and flavours have been created in this book. Some recipes are very simple to make, others take a little extra care but they will all give a lot of satisfaction – both to make and to eat.

Acknowledgments

Kind thanks to the management and staff of the Colchester Institute Centre for Hospitality and Food Studies UK – a Government designated Centre of Vocational Excellence – for their support and assistance in the production of this book.

Also, thanks to Josie Jones for her secretarial skills, Annabelle Reidy for baking late into the night and fellow lecturers Chris Barker, Tony Bending and Paula Summerell for their help and advice; and lastly, the following NVQ Level 3 students who gave up their spare time to assist: Michelle Hill, Brendan Timms and Simon Drain.